Up the Valley Down the Mountain
Based on a True Story

Write It Out
PUBLISHING, LLC

VIRGINIA BEACH, VA

Copyright © 2022 Tasha Moore, Up the Valley Down the Mountain

All rights reserved. No part of this publication may be reproduced, distributed, or transmitted in any form or by any means, including photocopying, recording, or other electronic or mechanical methods, without the prior written permission of the publisher, except in the case of brief quotations embodied in critical reviews and certain other noncommercial uses permitted by copyright law. For permission requests, write to the publisher, addressed "Attention: Permissions Coordinator," at the address below.

Contribution by Kiyanni Bryan, Write It Out Publishing LLC in the United States of America.

Illustrator: Maurice Rogers

Editors: Tamira K. Butler-Likely, Renee Johnson

ISBN:978-1-7377484-8-9

First Printing, 2022

Tasha La'Sheba Moore
Norfolk Virginia 23503
tmoore0328@gmail.com

Dedication

To all the people that have impacted my life, giving me lessons, knowledge, and love. Also, to my four wonderful children that I love unconditionally and vice versa. And I won't forget all the survivors of any abuse, illnesses, or generational curses. Let's tell our story to give another person strength to persevere. *-love TM*

Preface

When you hear the words "based on a true story," you more than likely think of how serious the story has to be. You think about the characters, their identity, and even some of the most heart-wrenching parts of the story have all got to be protected. Powerful, right? In that the impact of what you have gone through has a need to be protected because if left in the wrong hands, handled by the wrong individuals, it could be truly devastating to all involved.

These were the thought processes that I went through early on before deciding to tell and share "my story, my way." I have been questioned a lot and I even questioned myself, but in the end, I had to share my experiences. It was important to me not only to do so, but to do so in a way that everyone involved was protected.

Here I am as a write and here you are as you read. You are finding yourself face to face with another story and face to face with another survivor. Initially, I was leaning in that direction for my title, but not only did I survive, I endured and overcame some very traumatic things. With strength, determination, encouragement and faith, I was able to choose life. Conquering and overthrowing any and all obstacles and learning lessons that came my way. It would be so wonderful to have you on the same journey too.

Choices are hard but must be made, otherwise, you will stumble, trip, and fall down that valley, never reaching the other side. Allowing the baggage to cling to you instead of falling off, killing your purpose. That is one of the main goals and objectives of the adversary in our lives, that you never, ever fully reach your purpose. I knew early that is how it was set up for me if I didn't channel deep within.

The fact that I would never come to a full realization of who I was, why I was created, and that I do not use the fire for fuel to keep me going, to keep me encouraged when I wanted to give up and when I wanted to throw in the towel. It's been a roller coaster of a ride; hence, here we are, here we arrive. Here I share my story, Up the Valley, Down the Mountain, all based on a "true story." This is real, raw, and relevant to all survivors and speaks deeply to the spirit of abandonment. Journey with me as we deep dive into my story, my way.

Contents

Dedication	*i*
Preface	*iii*
Introduction	*vii*
Chapter 1: The Beginning	1
Chapter 2: Intensity	5
Chapter 3: Hard to Say Goodbye	9
Chapter 4: Choices	13
Chapter 5: The Start	15
Chapter 6: Realizations	19
Chapter 7: Lessons	35
Chapter 8: More of the Same	47
Chapter 9: Training Ground	61
Afterword	79

Introduction

The trust that we give to people early on when we are young children is by default. Especially those that are a part of our families and inner circle. As the trust seemingly grows, there are some close to us that not only abuse the trust, but they take advantage and abuse us as well.

Imagine as a child being extremely vulnerable and what feels like you're all alone. Now that there is a breach in trust and a violation, there is no one you feel like you can trust. You fall deeper and deeper into depression and despair, and everywhere you turn there is someone that adds to the abuse and turmoil. It hurts, and it's hard.

Seasons like this feel like they will never end, and they feel like they're placed in your life to single you out. It feels like God is not with you. This is where I found myself with various members of my family; this is where I remained for a period of two years that felt like twenty. Also, throughout my early years, tripping over every rock, I stumbled up the valley. This was my slide down the mountain (fast with no breaks). I honestly don't know how I made it through, but today I attribute it to the Most High. I didn't know Him the way I do today. I wasn't forced to have a relationship with Him until I moved in with my aunt and although it was another trip and fall up the valley with her, it was where my foundation in the word and in prayer began. It was there and even here today where it all started to make sense, although it was one of the hardest and most uncertain seasons of my life.

I share that with you in all the hardness and uncertainty, know that no matter what is being done and happening to you, the Higher is with you and He always will be. This is the first of my story, my way. This is the first of helping others free their hearts from their accusers; the first of me finally being able to exhale and focus on my assignment.

Chapter 1: The Beginning

My journey started with my mother Deloris. My mother and father came together and started dating back in 1978, shortly after his release from prison. Their romance progressed quickly and became toxic just as fast. The toxicity along with the fights and arguments led to their breakup. My mother had enough as she dealt with abuse, beatings, and even being hit by a car that knocked her into a ditch. All at the hands of my father Jonnie. My mother had her flaws also, not wanting motherhood and leaving me with my grandmother Lola, we also called her Big Ma when seeing fit to. Life for her was adventurous, on-the-go, bachelorette-style. Deloris was not interested in children, changing diapers, feeding, nurturing, or parenting. My father grew up with his great aunt, being separated from his siblings at a young age. My grandmother Sadie, often called "WARDEN," had gotten all seven of her children taken for reasons unknown. The other six were sent to foster care. After my father's great aunt died, he went out into the world on his own. At the age of eighteen, Jonnie faced a lot of challenges and hard times, leaving him channeled into survival mode all the time. The world was cold, and he was given no map as to how to live in it. Turning him tough, hard, and disconnected.

When I arrived into the world, the abuse was at an all-time high. They were abusing one another. Virginia Beach was home for us until one of the domestic disputes against Deloris caused Jonnie to be arrested. Finally, the split came when I was a toddler. Drug and alcohol abuse played a part in my mother and father's inability to parent me properly and with care. This was repeated behavior that my father also practiced in the lives of his other children and their mothers. Still, I loved my father deeply. My mind often wanders to the fond memories I have of him spending time on the weekends, going fishing and crabbing, and even on a few weekdays. My sister Queenie and I would go with my father to my grandma Sadie's house, and they would have us all playing while fresh fish and crabs would steam and fry. Those were good days that I love remembering, before the bad days. Yet and still, I had endured stories of his abusive life constantly as they were told to me over the years.

History repeats itself, they say, because the way my parents were raised constantly would show me why I suffered some toxicity and abuse (at their hands). Some things they just didn't know and therefore, I was unable to truly manifest in my own life. My mom was raised by her adoptive mother Lola and father Lester. Lola was close family of my mother's biological mother who had passed away from heart issues and high blood pressure stemming from alcohol abuse in a bathroom at a Christmas party was the story that was told. My Big Ma Lola did everything for my mom and it made her co-dependent and even self-entitled. My mom didn't know how to be self-sufficient, or how to be on her own. My grandfather Lester, who had worked for the city, was into alcoholism and became addicted to anything with alcohol in it (like cough syrup) gave my mother practically everything she asked for. My father walked a different path, not being raised with his mother and siblings. I always felt he never truly had anyone in his corner when he was younger, which may have caused his children to suffer. My father had to fend for himself in his teenage years and as an adolescent after he went out into the world. Staying in the streets taught him real life so quick. Survival as a teen made him stern and impassive. I can't honestly recall a time whereas I seen my father shed a tear. He cared about his family, but he showed it in his own way. The way he learned, the only way he knew. Even though he lived on the street, he would visit my aunts in their foster homes.

As he got older, his sisters supported him tremendously. They loved and adored my father, even though they knew his ways, because he was their protector. My father was strong, and he made it through every storm that came and passed. My father didn't take no slack and he always stood up for himself. I will say that is something he passed down to me, to stand up for myself and not be afraid.

In 1983, when my sister Queenie was born, we ended up spending entire summers at our Big Ma Lola's house. What started as a week, would turn into a whole summer and when I got old enough to comprehend, I understood my mother just didn't want to deal with the weight and the load of motherhood. Summers with Big Ma consisted of me learning how to cook and clean. Big Ma was hard working, wise and nurturing, and she always cared about others, and she was super selfless. For a period of four years I would go with my dad, but I would also experience anxiety from his breakup with my mom and my mom using me as a tool to hurt my dad, not allowing me to see him sometimes. My parents just couldn't see eye to eye. This caused us to suffer, as I have expressed, because of their disagreements.

Chapter 2: Intensity

My mother would go on to marry her second child's father Barry and they would stay married for about two years.

My mother would meet her third child's father in 1985. Although slightly younger than my mother, my mother's husband was a great guy who loved my mother. Deloris was leading a double life almost: staying out partying, seeing other men, and leaving for days and not coming back. Barry decided after a few years to call it quits. He tried to stay in our lives and had custody of us for a while, doing our hair the best he could and taking us to school, until the school realized something was off. I guess my stepfather couldn't do hair well and social services was called. Barry tried to convince my mother to allow us to stay with him so he could care for us after my mom came back for us; however, she had moved on with another man, and we were once again back in Virginia Beach after living in Norfolk for a few years. When we moved back with our mother and her boyfriend Charles, it was fun and family- like at first. It felt normal for a short time. We were going on outings and my younger sister's father, who was now in our lives, would step up for us when my mom tried to scold us. Then things escalated when he would give us treats randomly and frequently. I really didn't pick up on the fact that he was paying "special" attention more to me than Queenie at the young age I was.

One day, on a trip to the store, he put his hand on my thigh. I was unsure of what was going on (I was only eight), but I was scared. From there, we went home and continued on with the activities we were doing as if nothing happened, but life went downhill for me.

Charles started off as nice and kind and gained my trust with "little" things that would entice an eight-year-old.

Trust was also gained with my mom by intervening in discipline and telling her not to beat me. He would let her have a break from Queenie and I by taking us out or dropping us off at relatives' houses. While I thought he could be trusted and he was protecting and really had care and concern for us, he used a simple "piggyback ride" to slide his fingers into my underwear. It scared and confused me. I was only eight. How does an eight-year-old react to that? I never looked at him the same. I was afraid to be alone with Charles and I didn't know what to do. From visits to my room in the middle of the night, to offering my mother a break and driving me where I needed to go or to an appointment, I was completely isolated and away from people. Here was where he would reiterate what he would do to my loved ones if I ever told anyone what was being done to me.

My mom loved a good party and she loved to look nice. They called her Amazon because of her stature and her long legs. My mom also loved music and when she and Charles got together they did hard drugs, danced and drank and then she would pass out. Passing out for her meant an awakening for me, because he would take the liberty to come in my room and I would have to experience things I didn't quite understand, and I didn't understand why either. This went on for two years. As their lifestyle intensified, so did the abuse toward me. I was paralyzed with fear because he would threaten to harm my mom, my Big Ma, and my sisters if I told what was happening to me. When he tried to do something in front of my baby sister, I got the courage to talk to one of my school counselors. I didn't want the abuse to spill over to my other sisters because I didn't want them suffering and he was very abusive to my mom; so much that I would have to help my mom clean blood off the carpets and the walls while locking

Queenie in a closet so she didn't have to witness the abuse. Raven, my baby sister, was an infant to toddler when these things would be happening, so she would be sleeping or playing in the playpen. The abuse got so bad that I thought my mother was dying because blood was everywhere. I knew if I didn't tell someone and try to get help, the abuse and assaults would not have stopped. But courage came to me the day that I finally rose up and said something. I found the strength and confidence to let someone know what we were going through. I think about that life sometimes, how it would have been if I said nothing. I don't regret the choice. It got us away from the pain.

Chapter 3: Hard to Say Goodbye

In September 1990, my Big Ma Lola died. At the time, I was in school and started getting sad and lonely because my grandmother wasn't around to protect me anymore. I felt safe in her presence and in her home. My stepfather couldn't hurt me when I was over there. I knew when she died that things would change, which was why I worked up the courage to tell the guidance counselor. This was the day everything truly changed for me and my siblings. They kept me and my siblings that day, not letting us go home. With Queenie and I already in the system, we ended up in the hands of CPS. From there, I ended up staying with my paternal grandmother Sadie and my aunt Margaret. My siblings followed suit with their respective families.

From here, we were in the system via CPS (my sisters and I) and it was about a month before we saw my mom again. My sister ended up in the foster care system because her dad, in this case, was the abuser and she couldn't go with him. We were all separated. Even with this happiness of relief from all the hurt and anxiety, there was what felt like a dark cloud still surrounding our family. One of my sisters was sexually assaulted in foster care at the age of two, and the loss of my mother and not being with my siblings was all happening at the same time.

I was going through a lot mentally at this time, feeling like everything that was happening and going on was "my fault" because one of my sisters was suffering at the hands of an abuser in her foster home. If only I had never said anything to the guidance counselor, I thought to myself, then maybe my siblings wouldn't be in this situation. I was sad and fearful about it until we all ended up going with my mom's sister Wendy. My aunt Wendy lived in Indiana and at the request of my mom, came to Virginia to take us back with her to Indiana to care for us. Deloris didn't want us to be split up. This was supposed to be temporary while she went to rehab. In addition to rehab, Deloris was to also stay away from my abuser.

This was a tipping point for me. It was life-changing too, even though I was only eleven, being in the house with my aunt Wendy. It was a Godly home, but it was also abusive, in that we had a strict routine and I was forced to learn the Bible, which was something I never had to do or learn or something that was enforced in my life. My mom didn't take us to church, nor did we read the Bible since her lifestyle consumed her. There were times in the home when my aunt Wendy would go around and ask us to recite a scripture. I was blank, I didn't know what to say. It was hard for me to pray when I really didn't know what prayer was. My aunt began to discipline me because of this. My cousin Renee, we call her "Tootsie," told me when my turn came just to say, "Jesus wept." So, the next time my turn came, I said Jesus wept, and it must have been the right answer because my aunt moved on to the next child.

My other sister, in the same position as me, repeated the same thing I did, because she too didn't know the Bible. We would literally get into trouble if we didn't know scripture. Our aunt

Wendy took us in, but deep down, the more we were disciplined, it felt like she didn't want us. We weren't care for or loved. My aunt accused me of being possessed by the devil because she had no liking for my father or his family and believed they were of the devil and told my sisters not to talk to me. If they found themselves doing so, it was a negative consequence for them. I learned from that moment that it was going to be tough living with my aunt. Our daily routines would consist of various household chores that if not done right, would result in being disciplined. My aunt's mood for the day would also determine if we ate more than once or not that day, and we didn't have the liberty to go to the refrigerator because it was locked.

As you can see, my siblings and I endured a lot to be so young and innocent, not understanding why we were being mistreated. Regular church attendance was also required, and we were in church a lot! You see, my aunt Wendy was a deaconess who was very much respected in the church. No one at the church knew how my aunt was at home, except my other aunts.

Everyone else thought of her as a great Samaritan for caring for her sister's children. The church knew all that she did and sacrificed by taking me and my siblings in, and that made her highly respected. Inside, however, we were dealing with a lot of abuse and sadly, no one knew. My siblings and I hid it well, especially at church.

Chapter 4: Choices

When I was in middle school, I tried to find my way, so I joined a gang. I was enticed with the promise of someone being there for me, no matter what, someone having my back, and someone protecting me. In the moments before deciding to join, I really felt like I had no one. Hanging with my fellow gang members was what I would choose to do in these moments. We would find ourselves in dangerous situations. This ended for me suddenly when one of my friends was murdered. Jaquis, in the streets, it was "Jay," was not only my friend, but he was also my classmate and fellow gang member. This impacted me in a major way. I will never forget what happened that sadly changed our lives. Not to mention, we were just talking about him getting his life together, doing the right thing, getting our grades right, etc. I was traumatized because I knew in Jaquis's heart, he wanted to do better and be better, stop all the banging and live a life without chaos, but it was too late. Jaquis lost his life to gun violence at the age of fifteen.

When my aunt Wendy learned of my friend's murder, she immediately packed us up and we drove to Richmond in the middle of the night. Arranging for the rest of the belongings to be shipped. She had a sense I was hanging around with those kids at the park where Jaquis was gunned down at. We stayed in a hotel for a couple of days and shortly thereafter, we were blessed with a place (not sure how that happened so fast). Up until the time I graduated middle school, I was still going through abuse at the hands of my aunt, the person I thought would be my outlet from the abuse I suffered at the hands of my stepfather. The abuse consisted of me sleeping on the floor with no pillow or blanket and isolating my sisters from me as well. When other family came to visit, I was made to stay on the stairs while all the children played. I sat in silence thinking of games to play in my head. Alone again. People experience life's hurdles day to day, some with support, some without support. I am an example of triumph. I hope this journey gives you understanding and healing as I shed my layers of pain and betrayal to heal myself and encourage others. I would like you to take a moment, grab a drink (hot or cold) and listen to the survival and life-lessons that I have learned from. I will say this: ALL of it made me who I am today. The molestation that took place in my life, starting at the tender age of eight, was an extremely traumatic time for me. My mother ignored my hints and drug abuse kept her preoccupied, so my cries and my pleas for help went unnoticed. At twenty-two years old, I was finally able to not be afraid of the dark after many, many years. The anxiety and panic attacks leaving me paralyzed with the "PTSD" onset fear of someone coming in the room when it was dark was constant. I could finally turn off the lights and do something simple like close my eyes. The reason for this was a lot of my abuse took place at night when my stepfather would enter my dark room. At the time, I didn't know that I would be okay and I would be safe by simply telling someone. I always believed I would be the one in trouble. The young mind can be manipulated in such a heinous form.

Chapter 5: The Start

Allow me to go back for a moment, to something traumatic that occurred that sticks with me like fungus at the bottom of a tree. A memory from when I was four years old (pre-K) and we were living in Norfolk, playing in the back area of our school (we lived down in section 8 homes at this time). Low-income housing in these times didn't always have maintenance in certain areas as often as they would other areas, so there was some trash in barrels in the area of the playground at the school I went to. My friends and I were playing a tag game and I slipped and fell, and when I slipped and fell, a broken bottle was on the ground. I didn't know it then, but it cut my elbow so deep that you could actually see my bone. My teacher started screaming and panicking, calling for help, trying to figure out what to do. She called over her assistant that was also out there watching us as we played, and they took me into the nurse's office.

I'm not sure to this day why the nurse took a paper bag and crumbled it to get it soft, but instead of trying to get bandages, she stuffed the bag inside of my wound. Maybe they were in shock and disbelief that they were staring at my bone through a very large gash. I couldn't even feel the gash, so I think I was in shock as well. I was four and I had a big gash in my arm and I'm looking at it. I see it, I know it's open, I could see the bone, but I couldn't feel the pain and I don't know why. Deloris raced up to the school and I can recall us laughing about it before when I was older. I remember us talking about it so many times, how she was in such a rush to get to me that she actually ran up there. She didn't even drive after she heard what happened to me. That's the only time I can say that she expressed a motherly act, nurturing and loving, and I never heard or saw it again.

We ended up going to the hospital by taxi because she left the car at home. I ended up getting stitches and I was really proud of myself for handling it the way I did. It ended up healing over a period of time, but I got the scar still today.

When I was between eight and ten years old, my mother still had us, so this was shortly before we were taken by CPS, but I remember she partied hard. Our house almost caught on fire with me and my siblings in it. My mother, in a haste, put something on the stove and left, assuming that Charles was going to come back in time. But he ended up coming a little too late and everything went left-field from there. Charles went looking for my mom and it was getting smoky. My sisters and I were crying and very scared, and I ran out the house thinking about the fact that my two younger sisters were left in there. I opened the door and yelled for them to hurry and come out. Queenie grabbed Raven because she was in diapers (she was a year old at the time) and ran straight across the hall. I feel bad when I think about it sometimes because I didn't go back in. I yelled at the door for them to come out, but I was only under ten years old. I guess it scared me with the sirens blazing from the warnings of a fire. We all had on long T-shirts, no shoes and just waited for the people to come help us. I will never forget that time. It sticks out for many reasons, one being how my mom chose her other lifestyle over us. We needed her and she chose, on many occasions, not to be there.

In another incident, my mom had a friend, Ann, who was also our neighbor that stayed adjacent to us, who used to come and help us out sometimes, watch us, and also give us some food when my mom didn't have any money to feed us because of her habits. Ann came over after a brutal fight in our home and helped us clean up blood. I will always remember her simple, soft, re-assuring words to me, "It's going to be OK." She told us, "Y'all are going to be alright." At the time, I wondered if that was true, especially seeing as though I was so young. It was constant warfare in our house and being "ok" didn't seem like it could be reality for any of us. Support is vital. Ms. Ann was so supportive, even though she had her own three children. God sent a few friends in my life that were supportive and to this day, I have a special bond with all of them. I wish I could be close to them all like we were in the earlier years, because they played a part in me coping with what was happening to me at home in a lot of situations.

We hung out a lot together and that was a comfort for me. Let me give you a little backstory on myself before we go deep into my embracement. I had always liked helping people and working in groups. I was in the third or fourth grade when I was in the spelling programs, and I was the president of the class. I was the one the teacher would ask to help other kids with their work. I've always been an achiever, despite all the things I had going on. I don't understand how I managed to do that, but I always had good grades in school, honor roll and they never failed. I always tried to overachieve. I don't know if my mind just decided to channel out, or if it was just built into me like that. I love dancing as I can recall dance battles with friends and music being my heart. It is my therapy. Poetry is another passion. I loved writing little rhymes and verses when I was younger. Teenage years that was, when hip hop was rising up faster than ever. I was in Job Corps and I used to do the RAW talent shows. I always liked to express myself through activity, and that was one of the things that always got me through the storm. I actually learned how to express myself through therapy and positive mentors when I was fifteen or sixteen years old, after getting in serious trouble. In Job Corps, I learned more than just a trade in business technology. I learned communication, healthy communication, social skills, and accountability. Those skills helped me realize what steps needed to be formed for me to walk my path.

Chapter 6: Realizations

When I was in Job Corps, I started studying the 5% Muslim religion and I experienced and learned a lot about myself. I learned that I could be in control of my anger, my thoughts, my feelings, and my emotions. I also learned how to be humble. I was not humble at all before I studied this religion. I did a lot and I dealt with a lot of pain and rage, causing problems in my life with the law. I was raised in Christianity (Pentecostal). I was plagued with a lot of thoughts from when we were taken away from my mom. I took some of my Christian faith and some of the Muslim lessons and started trying to apply both in my life. Ethics and humanity overtook me and I started being more humble. The friends I was surrounded by also helped in a tremendous way. They kept me balanced because they were on the right path. Through this process, I was able to get my GED, even through being expelled from previous schools. This is how I ended up in Job Corps.

While I was in Job Corps with my friends, they would help me deal with times of anger, depression, and sadness. I would take my feelings out on people sometimes and my friends would support me in emotional ways. One of the closest friends I know, who was genuinely there without judgment, was Amina, a slim, chocolate, well-spoken individual that carried herself with great dignity, respect, and humbleness. We would have the most positive talks I had ever experienced. I wasn't used to a lot of soft tone talking and gentleness; let alone talks of knowledge, peace and love. I came to a solution for my issues with the help of Amina and Tyrique (a lyrical genius I often did rap shows with). "Ty" it was where we were at. I love them truly for that guidance. They would have me come to their homes on holidays and free weekends because I had no one to go to when I was in Job

Corps as far as Christmas break, Thanksgiving, and things like that. So, my friends started inviting me to their homes and that was the first time I say I really could feel another person's love whole-heartedly, other than the love with my boyfriend Dwight, known as "DREAD" and his mom Linda that never frowned upon me, however corrected and guided me. Dwight's grandmother "GMA NAY," also gave me learning tools that I still use today. Grandmother Naomi, "GMA NAY," a sweet giving, loving woman from the Caribbeans, taught me how to cook, at the age of thirteen, seafood dishes and Caribbean food. That was the first initiation to what love was for me in a family, but when I got the friends at Job Corps it was like we all bonded in a way from similarities. We were like this huge family that stayed on top of each other making sure we all were alright. They focused extremely hard on helping me get through the anger and coldness to graduate. They really wanted me to make it and we all shoot for the stars together.

I did end up getting into one situation where I almost was kicked out of Job Corps, but the people there did a deep look at everything that I had made and encountered. With some positive vouches from staff members, they decided that one incident was not as hard or intolerable, I'll say, as something irreversible, so they ended up letting me stay and complete my GED. I got my driver's license and a business technology certification at the age of sixteen and I graduated when I was seventeen, so that was a big accomplishment for myself because I really didn't even believe in myself at these moments. It was actually the encouragement and good energy of my friends, Amina with her long talks about life and the future, while my friend Tyrique was always talking about unity, loyalty, and trust. Trips home with passes for the weekend (always about #US) making sure that we all got together to motivate each other and be one another's support, got me through to press extra hard and prove that I was worth something

to myself. I always felt like I was nobody because it was told to me so many times by people that were supposed to care for me and guide me. They failed. I felt like, why am I here on earth? What am I here for if nobody loves me? I often wondered why nobody wanted to care for me or take care of me. I would ask myself this while trying to focus and get to my destiny. Why isn't there anybody in my corner?

Those are the types of feelings that I was experiencing around thirteen on up to seventeen, which was why I became suicidal at fourteen years old. I had also dealt with being a cutter, a person that will self- inflict his or herself with a razor, knife or scissors. Not being able to see your mother, father, and siblings all at once was unbearable for me. The cutting only eased the pain temporarily. I was using it as a coping mechanism when I got frustrated, angry, or felt pain. When somebody hurt me and I was upset, I would go in a closet, bathroom or my bedroom, depending on where I was during those moments, and I would take the scissors or a razor and I would just self-inflict and cry, letting out muffled screams with each cut. I'm glad that I ended up being able to overcome this trial, but you have to really pay attention to people that are dealing with this because it could be silently done like mine was. I almost succeeded one time with slitting my wrists. I thank God I am still here, but some people are not as fortunate. If you know anyone struggling with anything, try to guide them to the right place to get support.

When I graduated from Job Corps in 1997, I came back to where I was with my grandmother Sadie in Virginia Beach. I wasn't staying with her, but I was in that area. I ended up staying with my cousin's kids' mother Shyreeda, but everyone called her Reeda. She stayed in an area close to where the country was and I just tried to pick up the pieces of my life over at her house. What ended up happening was I began to care for my little cousins, making sure they were OK

and trying to help Shyreeda with the different mental struggles that she was going through. We were sort of like a yin and yang, and we depended and relied on each other. I remember I first met Shyreeda when I was twelve. She went to Job Corps with my cousin, Jayceon

a.k.a "JayBoog." This is, of course, before I went because I'm the youngest of the grandchildren on the girls' side of my grandmother Sadie's grandchildren. My cousin Winston is the youngest boy. My grandmother had nineteen grandchildren and she used to have some of them come to her house to stay when they were coming home for Christmas breaks. Jayceon would bring Shyreeda with him.

At those times, I was not feeling pretty about myself, even though I had a boyfriend (Dwight). I had old clothes from thrifty stores, old shoes (hand-me-downs), nothing new or in fashion. I wore what my grandmother Sadie and father could afford, I guess. Shyreeda would come around to do my face up with pretty makeup sometimes. She'd do my hair in up-do's and pretty, thick "Poetic Justice" braids, as they were called back then. She would go buy me some clothes to wear so I could look how young ladies were looking at the time in scrunchies, jean sets, fishnets and mesh. I must say, Shyreeda was a style guru. She would look me in the eyes with this great big smile, I'll never forget when I was thirteen, so impressionable, and say, "you're beautiful, you know that? You know that, right? You're beautiful." She would tell me that every time she came around and the more I heard that from her, the more I started having confidence about my face and body and what I looked like because I didn't think I was pretty back then. I was told I was ugly by my aunt Wendy so much, and the cutting of my hair for me to be humiliated had me believing that I was ugly, and I suffered low self-esteem.

Eventually, Shyreeda ended up moving in with us after she left Job Corps. So, when I left and came back, she had already been staying with my

grandmother Sadie for a while. She had already had one of her oldest children by Jayceon, and I think she was on her second child by him when I actually moved into her apartment. She had gotten popular in the beach area, making friends, exploring the city she lived in. And when I lived with her, she was still taking me on shopping sprees to keep me looking fashionable. She taught me how to do hair like plaits and cornrows, starting off with me just doing washes for her. She was a well-known beautician, unique and spiced-up, styling any type of hair, any type of style. Then, it went from that to me learning how to do braids. She would say, "here, this is how you can make you some money until you get a job or get on your feet." And I would take that into account and start braiding and washing people's hair. And maybe when she was all the way booked, she would give me some of her clients. We were like sisters for the most part, and she looked out for me every second that she had. And for that, I will forever be thankful.

Job Corps was a great place as far as learning things, having new experiences, and meeting new people. I really wasn't around a lot of people where I stayed with my grandmother Sadie. They called her "Warden" due to the fact that she carried a huge ring of keys swinging from her housecoats daily. Dwight and his family and friends are who I socialized with. I may have hung out with my friends from school here and there, going to sleepovers a few times when I wasn't with Dwight and his family, but it was mainly Dwight that I was with. Learning about eating healthy, reading, and keeping your space free of negative sources. Looking back, I think about how going to Job Corps gave me an opportunity to look at things from different people's views because we had different people coming from different states and cities into Job Corps trying to change their life around for the better, get a GED, a trade, and to be productive. And the people that I became friends with were very spiritual, were natural, genuine people. They studied

meditation and spoke on how to calm yourself, they ate healthy, not eating a lot of junk food, mainly seafood, fruits, and vegetables, no pork or beef, and very little chicken. I had never been around people that were so into the health of their body and mind. Gaining their friendship was God sent. After my peers helped me through some tough times in Job Corps, I began to cleanse my body and my mind, which was how I was able to focus and pass my GED and receive my trade in business technology.

After I graduated, I ended up reuniting with Dwight as he was being released from county jail. We stayed in some efficiency hotels together and he invited his family members (cousins) down for a weekend. When they came down, they didn't want to go by the rules or laws in the state we lived in. They committed a crime while they were down in the state. Dwight was driving, so he was facing time, looking at going to jail for 6 years. I was about to turn eighteen and I actually had tried to join the Army. I knew he had some court cases coming up again, and he would possibly be serving a long sentence. He wanted me to go and do something constructive so that I could support myself, so I went into Mepps, which is a kind of conditioning or screening for the military in Richmond. I passed the Mepps and I got set a date for Boot Camp around January 1998.

This particular story all happened around October 1997. I remember sleeping in the bed when he left that morning with his family members. They went out for the day and I remember waking up and it was late, and he still wasn't back, so I started calling his phone, but didn't get an answer. I called around to other friends we both knew to see if he was over there with them and they said no, they hadn't seen him since earlier that day. He had driven with his family members and went to run errands. I ended up getting a collect call from the jail and all I remember was him saying he was in jail, him and his family members,

for a crime that they were being accused of. He never came back after that. I ended up having to be subpoenaed to court at eighteen years old, which was a lot to go through. Knowing that your boyfriend was at the wrong place at the wrong time, and he could be in jail the rest of his life for being around people that had different ambitions than him was traumatic.

I had to testify because a person was hurt during the crime that was committed. They survived. I was the girlfriend of the driver, so I was there as a character witness. To be honest, the person that was assaulted was actually testifying on behalf of my boyfriend because he knew him and he was a great person to him. He was trying to explain to the courts that he knew that my boyfriend was not aware of what was going to happen, and he wasn't holding him accountable. Given that my boyfriend was the driver of the car when the crime was committed, he either had to testify in the case against his family members, or he could be held as an accomplice to the crime. Let's get more into that later, but I will tell you that was a very devastating time for me because I'd always had him in my corner. My boyfriend understood my pain. He saw me clearly. The raw me, rough but delicate, tender but tough.

In 1999, I met some friends that were adventurous and free-spirited.

Leena was from the Northwest. She had a humble, pleasant aura about her and I felt a sisterhood with her. Her other friend ended up being my friend also, CeeCee. I think she was about two years older than me. As I began to hang out with them, they allowed me to come and stay with them since I was sleeping on the couch at either Shyreeda's house, or over at Mami Ginette's (my friend Angelina's aunt). I stayed with Leena and CeeCee for about three months. I started hanging out on the bases because that's where they were going, and we met quite a few different people during that time. We also started to have parties with lady hosts, cooking, playing cards

and music, and women dancing. That's how we made a living as far as taking care of ourselves in the home. We did not have actual jobs during those moments. We would arrange parties for retirements and birthdays. Also, other parties for special requests.

I ended up meeting a guy on the base named Shymeek, who was tall and dark-skinned with a big white smile from New Jersey. I remember Dwight, who was still incarcerated at this time, telling me to tell him the truth always about meeting someone because when he did get sentenced, he was my friend before anything. He told me he knew I was young and he knew he had to go away for a while. He understood that I was younger than him and that I would want to be with another person. So he told me to just tell him the truth and he would always care and love me enough for that. He just wanted me to stay by him and be a genuine friend as we always were to each other, regardless of anything. He just wanted me to make him still feel human like writing, checking on him, seeing how he's doing, and that was what I did. I always stayed by him and he stayed by me. When I met Shymeek, I did continue to write to Dwight and see how he was. Him and his family had been so awesome to me over the years. I also communicated with his family members and Ms. Linda, his mother, on a frequent basis.

Shymeek and I started dating in 1999. Always Jersey bound, I visited his home more than once and we became quite serious. I dated him for two years, and there were a lot of different experiences with him that I hadn't experienced before in dating. A lot of toxic things began to show with betrayal, cheating, and lying. When I met Shymeek, he was actually with more than one woman without my knowledge, and actually, the friend that we also used to hang out with together was one of the women. He told me she was like his sister, and they just joined the military together because he was from the same area in

the North. Actually, she was just a girl he went to school with, and they both joined the military at the same time, and they had been sleeping together, and I did not know. I was in the dark, under the impression that she was his sister since that's what he called her. That was painful for me and I saw rage and anger come out of me again at that point.

I began to act out on it because my feelings were so hurt and I didn't know how to handle what was happening to me as far as me trusting somebody and allowing them to let me love them and they love me and then do me so wrong, misleading me and not being honest. I was very angry, bitter, and feisty, and I ended up getting into some kind of domestic, toxic relationship with him whereas we would fight, break up, get back together, fight, break up, get back together. During those times, he would be sleeping with different women and he would come back to me later, and I ended up getting a disease twice from that. Not a proud moment in my life, but it was curable and I survived. I still don't understand to this day why I kept going back to him. I don't know if I felt like I didn't want to lose him because I lost Dwight, the first person I felt love for and I just wanted to make sense of his actions, or if I didn't want to be alone again.

I can't begin to tell you often too many times, I was ashamed for going back after he kept treating me that way, but I did finally decide to end it all the way in 2001. I called it quits after going to New Jersey with him one time to stay and he nearly got himself killed messing around with his old stomping grounds where he used to live. Shymeek went back to his old neighborhood where his cousins were and got into a situation with me after having some drinks. He bust my lip and it was bleeding in the backseat of the truck. His family saw that and went off on him because they didn't like men battering women and they saw how he began to change after the first bottle of liquor. It got bad with screaming, yelling, cursing and large crowds moving towards the commotion. It had gotten to the point of no return. They took him over by the Hudson River and jumped him and said that they were going to throw him in the river. My heart was pounding, thinking about how it could end. I begged and pleaded with those people. I was so scared. I kept saying, "Please, I promise he's going to get out of town right now, just please, don't do that. I will never forgive myself if y'all do that because of me." And the guy from the crew let him and myself go. He said, "You need to go back home and get away from Shymeek. He got a lot of inner demons he facing. He drinks all the time to drown them out." He said it with concern.

Then he said, "He is putting his hands on you, you don't need him in your life. You too smart for that." I wasn't getting a lot of words of kindness in these times, so it was pleasant to hear. I took that advice into consideration when I made my choice.

We basically got a ride from his cousin back to the train station to catch the train back to Maryland. When we went back to Maryland, we ended up staying a couple of days at his mom's house, but she was not happy with us staying at her house and not being married because she was very religious. She didn't believe in you sleeping together without being married, so we ended up going to a shelter in Maryland and staying in there for about a month and a half. The type of shelter we were in would allow you to stay there and find a job, and then when you found a job, you would have to turn your check in after you cashed it. They put the money away and gave you a certain percentage of your check each week to get your necessities with. By the 30-day mark, you would have enough to put down on an apartment efficiency or rooming house, whatever your situation was.

So, that's what we ended up doing, finding a rooming house that was near his job with the money that he and I had saved up. I was working at a warehouse where we cleaned linen sheets and dining room sheets and things like hospital gowns and curtains. It was a linen press company. We got our first place together and we were not homeless anymore. I was homeless at 19 and 20 for a while when we slept in the car out in his mom's backyard, so I was happy when we got that shelter program. But, after we got the rooming house, we began to fight even more because we were on our own. I was nineteen and Shymeek was twenty, and it was like he had something triggering in his brain. I didn't know what it was. He would listen to a lot of music about depression and dying.

He listened to a lot of music that was talking about killing and pain. I really did worry about his mindset, but not enough because I liked music like that also. We were all listening to that music, so I didn't think of it like that. But what really got me was the fact that he liked to clean his guns a lot; disassemble, put them back together, and he just played with them a lot. He knew how to shoot well because when he was in the military, he got a high rank on his sharp shooting. He got discharged from the military because he broke a rule. He got kicked out, along with his best friend, which ending up being my niece's father later on down the line.

He would be cleaning the guns a lot, like an obsession, and it kind of worried me, like he had revenge on his mind. I didn't see anything else wrong with him except for, like I said, when he would cheat on me.

Then, I wouldn't want to be with him anymore and he would have an issue with that. We would end up fighting a lot, so eventually, I got tired of the fighting, the cheating and the going back and forth. He would be with me one moment, then the next day, sometimes hours later, he's with someone else. It took a mental toll on me. Imagine the seesaw effect that I created with that choice.

One minute he would love me and ask for me to stay, and the next minute he was with someone else like I was an option. It was so hurtful and confusing at the same time. So, when we had that last fight, it was because we had just broken up a week prior and he had moved back in with his mom, I guess. I'm not sure where Shymeek went exactly, but I know we weren't living together anymore. I went out for the Fourth of July with my friends for a night and when we got done watching the fireworks, having a gathering, and eating and things, I went home, where I lived on the other side of town. I had gotten my own rooming house by this time, but he would still come stay with me. It was literally like walking distance from my house to my friend's house. I really didn't have to catch a cab or anything because I could walk in less than 15 minutes. By this time, we had split up so many times with the other rooming house we got when we left the shelter that I ended up leaving him and going to get my own. I stayed with a friend until I was able to do that; someone I worked together with at the linen warehouse.

Shymeek ended up coming back to move in with me, but the room was actually in my name because I never wanted to have to go through being kicked out in the middle of the night in the snow again. Have your own. Always have your own, I thought. I was walking up to my door and

I'm hearing music, but I'm in a rooming house, so I thought it was my downstairs neighbor. I open the doors and I see his friends in there. I hear them say to him that I'm home and I'm looking like what's the problem. I see a girl come out of the house and that's when I asked everybody to leave and they all walked out. I told Shymeek, "No, you're not going anywhere." I closed the door behind him and we proceeded to get into an argument about why he was at my house and why he had another female at my house. I asked the female who she was there for and she told me she was there for Shymeek. So, after this big fight right here, I ended up getting my lip lacerated on the side from when he punched me. I packed my things in the middle of the night and got a ride, paying someone to drive me back to Virginia.

I made up my mind that night that it would be the last time I went through any of that turmoil again with him. I felt that I was too young to be having those types of experiences and I was tired of being hurt, lied to, deceived, and then having to deal with the mental aspect of it. It was a time in Shymeek's relationship with me that I was in the hospital from a mental breakdown, about to be committed, believe or not, and that's just not where I wanted to be anymore. Vulnerable, defeated, lost. When I think about the reality that I am just not myself because of someone else, I said, "NO." I could do it no longer. So, when I came down in the middle of the night, I ended up knocking on Queenie's door and I said, "I'm going to need a place to stay because I want to start over. I don't want to go back." And, of course, everybody thought we broke up and got right back together all the time, but I was finished, done. I walked away this time. I chose me. I asked Shyreeda not to tell him where I was at all because I was done, and she respected my decision. He, in fact, called and drove down here twice to be exact. How toxic is that? To come to Virginia to find me. After deceiving me time and time again, breaking trust. I did not respond because I just was tired of being in that type of relationship with Shymeek and I didn't want to keep repeating those ways anymore. Enough was enough.

I remember when he did the last drive down, it was like the end of July. He drove down twice between the Fourth of July and the end of July 2001. Shyreeda said that he had come by and tried to get the information on where I was, and she just told him she didn't know. She said that he had said to tell me he really loved me and he really was sorry. Broken record playing, I heard. That was the last thing I heard about him until September 2001. My friend, Larissa still lived up there and she called me and asked me did I hear anything about Shymeek and I said, no, I didn't hear anything about him. She told me that he was on the news. He had done the unthinkable. He had gone to his friend's house and some kind of confrontation happened between him and another person there. He ended up putting a pillow over that person's head, shooting them in the head and going back to work like nothing happened.

I said to Larissa, "What if I would have stayed with him? It could have been me." I said he snapped from the conditioning of a soldier's mentality to a menace. It scared me, just the thought of those times we were fighting. He always cleaned his guns and kept them in bed, one under the pillow, and one in the closet. I just thought to myself, I was playing with fire, but I lived fearless. My friends seemed to think he just snapped after he couldn't get in touch with me and get me to come back to him on top of all the other things he struggled with inside. That was the tip of the iceberg. I was gone. Him knowing I was never coming back. Literally, it was two months after I refused to respond to him, or take any of his calls, or let him know where I was that he committed that act. It sent chills up my spine knowing that he had that type of mentality in him the whole time and I didn't know it was there brewing up. But I am so thankful that I'm still here and the person he shot did not die. They survived. But he still got twenty- five to life for that. I don't know if it saved another person possibly from him doing that type of action to them too.

I'm just thankful that I'm here to still talk instead of being six feet under.

Chapter 7: Lessons

I have so much to share, so much to give as far as learning lessons as well as encouragement. By now, you know my childhood was not the best for me, but I embraced the truth and reality of what I went through to heal and grow further into my purpose. About three to four months after living with our relatives and my baby sister in foster care, my mother called her sister, Wendy in Indiana and asked her to take all three of us so we could stay together. Her sister said yes. Wendy came down to court and got documents to gain guardianship, then took us back to Indiana. At that moment, I was almost twelve, I believe. I was nervous, thinking about what things were going to be like. We had not seen Aunt Wendy in a couple years. She would come to Virginia to visit at least once or twice a year. We didn't know Aunt Wendy that well, but we knew she was our aunt. Hoping for change and a better life, I was happy to be with my sisters again.

Let me take you to the time when my sister was about four, we were living with my aunt Wendy and Raven fell off the top bunk of the bed and busted her lip. It was bleeding pretty bad and I tried to hold her and console her like a big sister does. My aunt came in the room and snatched my sister out of my arms and said to me, "Didn't I tell you, you can't be around her." She made me go back to the bathroom, where I sometimes slept on the floor with no blanket or pillow; no nothing; just the cold floor. Pajamas wasn't enough warmth, especially in the winter. Or, I would have to sleep in her room at the foot of the bed, still with no blanket or pillow. I was also made to sit on the stairs while my sisters and cousins played. They wanted to interact with me, but that wasn't allowed, so I just looked on while sitting on the stairs daydreaming. I would pretend I was out there playing with them and a small smile would crack, then reality would sink in with the slam of the door. A couple of times other family members came by and they saw how she treated me, but they turned their heads to it. "HUSH, HUSH, don't speak about family business." That's what was told. "BE QUIET. DROP IT." Blind eye to it. "We family. Family don't speak on family." All taught at an early age to just keep quiet. That was torture for me because I didn't understand what I was doing wrong. And I didn't understand why I had to be separated from all the other children, but I just did what I was told because I didn't want to get in trouble.

I remember my aunt Veronica came down one summer, she and her sister with her kids, and they were all playing like always when they came down to visit. All the children would go in the backyard to play dodge ball and tug of war; all the fun games to play when it is nice outside, and you have a lot of people. I was sitting on the stairs by myself when Aunt Veronica came up to use the bathroom. She slipped me a cheeseburger because they had McDonald's downstairs, but I couldn't get any, and she told me to go in the bathroom and hurry up and eat it.

Then, Aunt Veronica gave me a few dollars and said to get me some snacks later when I had the chance. After school normally, my aunt Wendy would arrive home a few hours after us. I unwrapped the cheeseburger and ate it in the bathroom and she took the wrapper back so I wouldn't get in trouble. But see, that's the thing, we tend to sweep a lot of things under the rug. She wanted to helped me but didn't know the way to help because remember, "Family don't speak about family business." I'm not blaming her or anybody else because it's not their fault. That is the way we were conditioned, to keep family business to ourselves. I just want the cycle to be broken on all of that, so we can evolve. It is possible. It was roughly a week later when I went to the store with the money my aunt Veronica had given me.

It was my favorite corner store near the house. I got a cold soda, a pickle, and a bag of chips. I didn't finish my soda and I left the bottle on the table in the kitchen, not thinking about the consequences. When my aunt Wendy came home from work, she saw the soda bottle and asked where I got it from. I told her I bought it at the store, and she said I stole it. I said no, I had money, and she asked where I got the money from. I told her the truth, my aunt Veronica, but she said that was not true, and she began to beat me with the cable cord. That's when I ran out of the house and down the street to the pay phones at the corner store and called for help. I dialed zero and the operator connected me, and that's how I was able to get to my grandmother's house, Grandma Sadie.

CPS contacted my dad to let him know that they had opened a case on my aunt Wendy. However, they did not take my sisters, and I thought that was odd since they had seen the abuse on me. What they told me was they could not prove that the scars my sisters had were from being abused; it could've been from them falling, it could've been from them playing and things like that. Child Protective Services were saying since we were younger kids, kids fall and hurt themselves, so they said they couldn't prove the abuse. That was a blow to my gut because I thought that when they saw the bruises on me they would take all of us from Aunt Wendy because she had been abusing all of us, but they said that was not possible at that time. My younger sister, Raven was devastated. She even started trying to pack her clothes while I was packing. "I'm so glad we get to leave here," Raven said as she grabbed her shoes out the closet. Tears began to fill in my eyes. My heart ached. "I'm so glad we are getting out of here so we won't have to be beat on anymore and Auntie keep being mean to us." Raven said as she stuffed her clothes from the drawers in a bag. I was crying as I was taking her clothes back out of the bag, trying to put them back in the dresser and explaining to her that she couldn't go with me. At this moment, she was around five and she wasn't really understanding that she had to stay. After about my fourth time putting Raven's stuff back in the dresser, she registered and realized that she wasn't going. We cried together, I gave her a hug, the biggest hug I could, I held her tight, and I told her I would never, ever, ever forget her or leave her alone. I told her I'll be right there every time she needed me. I started writing Queenie and Raven letters each week once I found out where they were, trying to teach them new school things. I would give them problems to solve, math essay questions, multiplication, and I would send the answers in the mail the next day. I would send all the different worksheets I made by hand first, then the next day I would mail the answers to the worksheets. When I look back now, I observe the fact that my intelligence at thirteen was great to even do that, but I did it. So, my sisters kept in touch with me too by mail. They would send me little notes and smiley faces when they would send the answers back. My cousin, Renee "Tootsie" (one of Aunt Wendy's daughters) would help them send letters to me. I remember being sad when CPS took me out of Aunt Wendy's home, thinking I would never be around my sisters again. My aunt Wendy tried to keep us apart because she still believed my family was no good, but it never worked. I found her every time she moved. There would be people in the streets who knew both sides of my families and they would say where my aunt was staying, and I would go over there, of course, when she wasn't home. Back then, most of our families stayed in clusters in different housing areas, so my father's side of the family would be living in the same housing areas as my mother's side of the family, and I would go over to my paternal family's house and I'd see my sisters outside on the porch. I would go over and give them some money for shoes and things like that, and just try to check on their welfare. By this time, I'm not so innocent anymore. The hustle and street life are what I'm starting to learn by default. How did I end up here? No rules, no authority, no guidance, or guidelines. I could do things most thirteen-year-olds could not do like drinking and not going to school with no repercussions. The words "no" or "you cannot" don't exist anymore.

I can tell you one way I ended up on that path. See, when we moved with my aunt Wendy after being taken from my mom, the agreement that I was aware of, even though I was eleven when I heard it. I eavesdropped and heard my grandmother speaking with my sister Queenie's aunt about the court proceedings. The agreement was we were supposed to stay with my aunt Wendy while my mother Deloris got her self-treatment for the drug addiction. She was supposed to stay away from my stepfather and try to find housing again and get us back. The judge gave her six months to do that, but my mother did not gain custody of us back. She ended up moving to Indiana to be closer to us with my grandfather Lester, who had dementia. By this time, my grandmother had passed in 1990, remember? When my mother moved to Indiana, she ended up letting my stepfather move to Indiana with her. I had those moments I really was confused on why because she knew what the allegations were. She knew what I had told the school and yet she still allowed him to come and stay at her home. So, with Deloris not complying to the courts, we did not go back and actually, she never got custody of us back.

I ended up joining a gang while I was living with my aunt in Indiana as I spoke of earlier. I got jumped in by five boys. I was a tomboy back then, getting into fights with boys, jumping gates, climbing trees, wrestling; it was normal to me. I began to do activities that gang members do, and I was putting the family at risk multiple times. They would come to the house and break the windows and try to steal from the house and cars. What a dice game I was playing as a teenager, so naïve and easily influenced, but that is one part my young mind wasn't processing. Where I was putting myself at risk, I could've ended up dead.

Remember when I told you about losing a friend right in front of my eyes at the park when he was fifteen? We hung around the same group and he didn't want to gangbang anymore and I was listening and leaning toward the same. It was getting rough out in the streets, and we were losing people, three to four at a time some days. I had given Jaquis some tutoring lessons in math and history a few weeks before he was gunned down, and he was talking about how he wanted to leave in the spring when spring break came around and move down to Texas where his father's family was from. Jaquis' father had been serving a life term since he was four in an Indiana State Penitentiary and Jaquis stayed in contact with his father's family. He would go visit his aunt, sister and grandmother in the spring and summer. He started doing good and getting good grades so he could work towards becoming a truck driver and right before spring break, that's when the altercation happened at the park.

Some boys from the opposite gang saw me walking Queenie to the candy lady and jumped me at the store. I told Queenie to run home because I didn't want her getting hurt. I kept the full cans of soda I had bought and tied the bag and defended myself. After it was broken up, I went back and told my best friend, Detron, who was a part of the gang that I was in. We were in the same grade, rode the same bus to school, and we both moved from different states to Indiana. We became friends from not knowing anybody else. Detron called up Dusty and Benny. Things got out of control quickly. With things escalating at the school, fights in the hallway, words thrown across the room, everything ended up at the park where the shootout began. That's when Jaquis got shot in the back of the head and the bullet came out through his eye. Trauma hit me like a sack of coins across the face as I watched the fatality. I was upset and angry because all I knew was that he wanted to change. He didn't want to run in the streets anymore. That just stays in my mind. Cause and effect.

Every action has a reaction. The moment when that occurred, it was broadcasted on all of the news stations. That's when my aunt Wendy decided to pack us up in the middle of the night and drive us back to Richmond, Virginia. She did that because she knew that I had started affiliating with the gang and she thought that it would be best to leave before they retaliated again.

At that time, Richmond was named the most violent homicidal city in the US and for some reason, I wanted to dib and dab in that danger, as my father would say, "living on the wild side." I was very young and stubborn, acting out my pain. I did end up getting into some gang activity down that way in Richmond also. I was jumped in eighth grade right before graduation by four boys. I held my ground. It wasn't like I'd got beaten badly. I knew how to protect and defend. My father was a mild weight boxer for years in the penitentiary and he had been training me since I was five. Being the youngest of nineteen grandchildren will make you tough also. Rolling the memories back, I think about all the dangerous things I did and got myself into at such early ages. Instead of playing video games, going to the malls and movies, I was skipping school, drinking, in the streets, running from the pain and hurt of having no love at home and being abused. This fight happened right when school was letting out. Shortly after is when I went to live with my father, Jonnie. Jonnie ended up getting custody of me at thirteen. I moved back to Virginia Beach and my father made an agreement with my grandmother, Sadie that I would go to school from her house. He felt like her house would be a better place for me to get an education versus where he lived in Chesapeake at the time and he would get me on the weekends.

After a while, I realized that he was not really going to be keeping up on that arrangement. Grandma Sadie began to resent me because my father Jonnie was not doing his part. That was another devastating time for me because I had already been abused from ages eight to ten by my stepfather, then got taken away and moved in with my mom's sister so we could all stay together and ended up being abused again. Now, I'm over with my grandmother on my dad's side and she started being verbally abusive telling me how my mother and father didn't want me, nobody wanted me and how I should have never been born. I feel it was out of frustration because she didn't want to raise any more children. I was her nineteenth grandchild, the youngest, as I told you. She was tired and I only recognize that now.

Back then, I was hurt by it all. I felt helpless and angry. Angry that my father wouldn't pick me up as often. Angry that my mother was not fighting to get me back. I couldn't understand why everywhere I went, nobody wanted me. I was a burden; extra baggage. I was being beaten and belittled. Sometimes the things that were said would make me feel ashamed of being alive. I began to cut myself at that point with razors. In moments of frustration, I would try to end it. The final thing that I did at my grandmother Sadie's house as far as trying to bury the pain, was when I took some pills, which I did almost die from. My sister Monise was picking me up that weekend so I could get away for a little while, and I took some pills that my boyfriend Dwight had left. He had some pain pills he was taking for pain from a car accident and they were in his book bag, so I went in and took them. I didn't feel anything in the beginning, then I started to walk slower and feel my body getting heavy as I was packing my bag and going towards the living room. Monise picked me up and I got in the car with her and I lost consciousness. I couldn't move or do anything else, but I could hear her trying to wake me up. I could hear her telling her husband to turn back around. It was faint and muffled. We raced back to my grandmother's house, driving as fast as they could around the winding country roads. Pitch black darkness, no sidewalks or guard rails; only deep ditches.

They took me out of the car and laid me on the floor right at the door while Monise called 911. The paramedics came and they were assessing me and asking questions. I could hear them trying to get more information on me from my grandmother and sister, and my grandmother stated to let me die because she had insurance. When she said that, the paramedics said to her, "You should not be saying things like that about your granddaughter. That's probably why she did what she did. I'm going to get her some help." And they also reported the lack of concern to the hospital for social services to follow-up on. Cries for help, I thought. I had already started getting in trouble in school; fights in the bathroom and locker searches from the security randomly done looking for knives, skipping classes and school. I was acting out and not doing well because I felt like I was alone. I felt like I had no one. When they pumped my stomach and I had to be monitored and watched for three weeks making sure I was woken up often and healing on bed rest, I ended up asking Dwight to let me go over where he was, which was his grandmother Naomi's house. I ended up going to stay over there for a little while, just to make sure I was okay and just to be at peace for a little while from all the hurt and the pain. His grandmother Naomi was very nice to me, and she treated me just like I was one of her grandchildren. She would go to Belize every summer and bring back seafood, huge lobster tails and shrimp for me. She taught me how to cook the proper way from scratch instead of microwave nuggets, french fries, and chicken patty sandwiches all the time. Those were my favorite foods besides seafood. It was easy to fix and I didn't need to eat a lot of those foods to be full. She told me, "You must cook. You must learn. That's part of what women learn to do is to cook and make sure that their family is fed." And so, she started teaching me how to make island food and fresh meat marinades. I left her home knowing everything about fresh seasonings, fresh cooking, and taste testing. She was one of the most positive people that I knew at that time. The most warming feeling about her in my life was the example of kindness and guidance because I felt like somebody finally cared about me. "GMA NAY" as we called her,

Dwight, and Ms. Linda were like angels in my presence when I wanted to end it all. I really truly appreciate the fact that they came across my path to help me understand that love is possible and people can care about you.

The story of how I went to Job Corps will tell you how encouragement, support and understanding really goes a tremendous way. I ended up going to Job Corps because Ms. Linda suggested that it would be a great idea to keep me out of trouble and so I could have an education. By this time, I had already gotten expelled from high school for a fight that ended up with blood on school grounds. That is why they expelled me from the schools in Virginia. Ms. Linda decided to get assistance with getting me an education by taking me to a group home. Ms. Linda didn't have any paperwork on me for any guardianship, so she said the best thing to do was to allow the group home to sign me into Job Corps. I was very reluctant. I felt like I was being pushed away again and I felt like I wasn't wanted again, which, in fact, wasn't the case. She just wanted me to have an education and be self-sufficient, but at that moment, I felt abandoned, so I ran away from the group home about two weeks in and tried to go back to my mom's house (Ms. Linda). I called her my mom because she was like a mother figure to me. She was concerned and she communicated well with me. I cried so hard. I was so confused. I asked why I couldn't stay, why they didn't want me, and she was very nurturing with her answers to me. Ms. Linda expressed that it was important for me to get an education so that I could become something one day. Once she really broke it down, I understood. I did end up going back to the group home to be enrolled in Job Corps. I was signed in through the state. I ended up being a ward of the state because my guardians at that moment, my grandmother Sadie, and my father Jonnie, didn't sign the paperwork for me to get into the school. So, the state had to take over guardianship so they could put me in the Job Corps program (a program for people that have been expelled from school, dropped out of school, or getting in trouble and needed a new path). That's when I met Amina, Tyrique, Gizelle, Jamal, and a few others that were even more spectacular. As far as genuine love and honesty, these special people reiterated the fact that there were people out there that cared. We made a tight bond with one another. Near and far, we are still friends.

Chapter 8: More of the Same

I want to take you back some time ago to where the most traumatic things were happening to me at the most vulnerable, transforming times. I was becoming a teen, my hormones were changing and I had confusion and curiosity. Trying to find out who I was as a person was seeming so difficult. I knew I had to grow up one day. Are these the things I do to others (hurt and abuse) when I grow up? I thought to myself. I was so young and inexperienced in life skills and what living a "good" life was about. I can recall one moment when I was growing up with my grandmother Sadie after being taken from my mom's sister, Aunt Wendy the summer of '93. The first day that I arrived with my grandmother, I was thirteen and it was a little bit before school. I think it was August 1993. I was happy to go live with my grandmother Sadie because I remembered all the times me, my sister Queenie, and my cousins had when we would spend the weekends at her house having so much fun. She would always buy us candy and ice cream. When in season, steamed and fried crabs it was. I was very happy because I finally did not have to be abused and mistreated by my aunt, sleeping on floors without blankets and pillows, hit with broom handles or cords and getting my hair cut off, walking around with it shaved low like a boy. The only way you could tell the difference with me and the boys was when I wore earrings or dresses when that happened to me. The humiliation caused the anger and aggression in me when I was going to middle school. If I only knew to embrace myself as I know now. I learned with growth.

I thought my grandmother Sadie was going to be a change in my life for the better. However, when I tried to fix her something to eat, I saw someone I had never been around before. Grandma Sadie wasn't like she used to be when I was younger. I look back and I think this was my third day there. I had made her a fresh salad and brought it to her and she immediately yelled at me, "What did you do to my food? I'm not eating that! You can take that back and throw it away." I was very shocked because I couldn't understand why she thought I had put something in her food. It hurt my feelings so bad when she told me to go throw it away and that she was not eating anything from me because she knew I had put something in her food.

Now that I am older, I realize that she was starting the onset of dementia, but at the age of thirteen I didn't realize it. I didn't know anything about the medical field, even though when I was little I used to want to be a cardiovascular doctor. But then, I thought about it at that time, and blood was not on my list of favorites, so I changed my mind. I knew that I could not be precise enough to work on someone's heart and the consequences if you make a mistake. So, then I wanted to go and study law when I was around 10 years old, then I thought about that type of career and I said no, I can't do that either because I don't want anyone coming after me if I win or lose a case. That can go both ways in those scenarios. A person can be mad because you got the defendant off or they could be mad you did not get the defendant off. There's two sides to every story on that. So, I came up with business, and that was when I was in Job Corps. But, back to the story of my grandma Sadie.

Before she had to take care of me, I was coming around and just staying over for summers, holidays and on weekends when my dad could get a chance to get me. My grandma Sadie was so nice to all her grandchildren as I could remember back when I was smaller, around seven years old. She would have family cookouts in the summer with generations of bloodline coming in from all over the United States. What is a good cookout without fresh fish fried straight out of the water, 90's music playing (one of my favorites was "SUMMERTIME", by Will Smith), and kids laughing and playing red light, green light while the adults played cards and drank Colt 45s or Old English. We had all of that going on. Real bonding, keeping the generations close with these gatherings. I feel now that I am older, my grandmother Sadie did the best she could do with what knowledge she had on how to raise children.

The toxicity I experienced while I stayed with my grandmother Sadie was at elevated levels. Not only was I being verbally abused by my grandmother, but when I would try to tell my father about it, she would deny it and say she do not know what is wrong with me and why I am making up lies. So, it was frustrating trying to tell my father what was happening. He would never see it, so he didn't believe it.

She used to have me keep my door open with the lights off when my boyfriend Dwight was not around and mind you, I am a teenager. I know that I shouldn't have had a boyfriend at that age anyway, but without the proper guidance, structure, and authority, I was able to do that. So, when he wasn't around, I had to keep the door open and all the lights off and that's when those moments really had me questioning the spirituality world because I would feel and sense a presence standing over me. I would keep the sheet over my head and I would just pray to God to cover me, protect me, and give me strength. My grandmother Lola before she passed, used to talk to me about afterlife and spirits and how to pray and keep faith, relaxing your mind and allowing no fear. I really do not know whether there was someone standing over me or not, but that presence in the room that I was sensing was strong, and it would happen all those nights that it was completely dark. I couldn't see anything on nights that I had my TV on and the doors closed. I had no issues at all, so I do not know if it was my grandmother Sadie. I could never tell you otherwise, but it was a presence that I felt, and I would just keep my head covered until the morning.

I wasn't allowed to play with the neighbors' children back then either because word around the town was my grandmother Sadie was a witch. I think they said that because she had this mole on her face up on her right side between her nose and cheek that looked sort of like those sketch pictures of witches. And her grayish eyes may have been scary to people because they were so cold and piercing. Being in her household not being able to socialize with certain people was upsetting. I wanted to go play volleyball or up the street to hangout and listen to music, but with us living where we were, that was not happening. I remember one night, late night around two thirty or three o'clock in the morning, trucks ran up in the yard and my grandmother Sadie, "Warden" if you asked around, went and got her shotgun. They were revving the engine in the yard and screaming and hollering curse words; words I do not wish to repeat. She kicked the screen door open with her legs and cocked back the shotgun and yelled out, "Alright, you get out of here! Get out now or I will put a hole in ya." She told me to get behind the couch. I was terrified not ever living through a moment with racism. I read about it, but I know my grandma Sadie went through it. How in the 90's we still have that frame of mindset? I was fourteen. It was puzzling. I guess it never ends. I closed my ears and my eyes and waited for her to tell me to come out. It seemed like eternity before I was able to come from behind the couch. They did pull off and leave. I do not know what it was about. I don't know if it was racial or not. It was Caucasian people from town that pulled up in the yard. Then it was the story of the land that my other grandmother on my mother's side (Grandma Lola) owned for years. I do not know if they just wanted the property. I never found out. The property and land are sold now. It is just field and construction where the house used to stand.

Staying at my grandmother Sadie's was a trying time because I loved her, but I couldn't understand her. I couldn't understand why she was treating me so badly when she used to be the sweetest person to me and now, she was doing some things that I felt were very abusive to a child. And to an adoptive child that she had under her care also. She would not feed him any meat and when he did eat, most of the time it came straight out of the can. Cold, not warmed in a pot or microwave. There were times I saw her have him take the food out of the woodpile, dishwater and garbage can and was made to eat it. He had to sit back at the table with that food, no matter how moldy and old it was. My stomach is getting nauseous talking about it because I couldn't help him and that was the most petrifying thing I had seen. I watched him be abused, but I tried to help him in some ways. I even snuck him some meat sometimes and I did say things to my grandmother Sadie, which she would say I was being smart mouthed. I would try to stand up for him and try to advocate for him, but nothing happened in that matter until after I was gone from the house.

He did eventually get taken out of the home too, several years later. I was glad to hear it when I found out. Eventually, my grandma Sadie had crossed the line for the last time. She had struck the little boy in the head and Child Protective Services were called. From my understanding, a family source said my aunt Hazelle called. He is actually a striving young Black man now that I heard. I'm not for sure about his psychological thoughts, however, considering what he survived. I have not been around him to know, but I'm sure he has some type of affect from that. I definitely deal with PTSD significantly from the trauma of being at my grandmother Sadie's house, being with my aunt Wendy, and even being with my mother Deloris. I struggle with that issue. Healing, becoming positive and wise every day I embrace and shed off the layers of hurt, pain, abandonment, and trust issues. Acknowledgement was the first layer for me.

I was constantly around violence. The type of violence you might think you only see on tv or in movies. When I was living with my grandmother Sadie she had a boyfriend, Robert at this moment, and he would have to stay in the room with the door locked on the outside. We would joke around sometimes calling my grandmother "Warden" because she had a set of keys that jingled right on the side of her housecoat. She would have the ring of keys safety-pinned to her gown with different keys up there. I don't care how many keys were on that ring, she always knew which key went to what. She was never confused about what key went for each door, car, or closet when it came time to choose one. She would padlock Robert in the bedroom and he was able to come out when she needed to go run errands, or when it was time to fix her food or give her medicine. Other times, he was able to come out to do yardwork or clean up the house. Robert would never give eye contact and he would speak briefly to be polite.

Then, he would have to go back to the room with one of those big fifty gallon buckets that he could use to use the bathroom until he was able to come back out. A couple of times he got out of line, that's what my grandmother Sadie felt like anyway, and she threw boiling hot water in Robert's face and his skin peeled off; second and third degree burns. It was pinkish red for almost a year. That was horrific for me, watching him go through that type of pain. But, for reasons I could not explain, Robert never left. He stayed through years of pain. The years of uncertainty and the cycle of abuse and fear is unbroken.

In another incident, she took a hammer and hit him in the mouth with it because he didn't agree with something they were talking about at that time. I just remember saying to myself, "These are some crazy things," feeling curious and shocked all at once. Is this how I should be? I questioned. Or should I be kind and patient and learn humbleness and control? I asked myself. Not knowing that over time I would learn just that. I did not understand why my grandmother Sadie was so angry. I never understood the anger she had because she had a sweet side to her, but that other side would come out from time to time. Now, flashing back on it, I know mental health is very, very real and it's not talked about a lot. Maybe my grandmother Sadie suffered from mental illnesses that was not diagnosed. I can't tell you, but I really honestly think she was ill because she went through a lot in her childhood and life from being raised as a mix of Indian and Caucasian. And Caucasian people tended to do racial things to her back then, so maybe she kept that hurt, pain and abuse inside. And bottling it up for so long, turned it into a force to be reckoned with. And as the cycle continues on through generations, I became a part of that cycle. I ended up becoming violent myself from watching. I just fell into the life of the streets and violence. And opening the door to that part of my life is when I ended up getting expelled in high school after only completing six months of ninth grade. I had shed blood on school grounds and I was on my final warning before being suspended indefinitely. The girl that I got into an altercation with fell on the ground when I got her off me. She hit her head and it started bleeding, so they expelled me.

After that, I was hanging out with Dwight and the friends that we knew together. We would just chill overall in Virginia Beach, and my best friend Christina, at least I thought she was my best friend, decided to betray me. She messed around with the guy that I was with; the guy that I had always known as a true friend and the guy that I felt was my protection at the moment because he and his family were there for me. I was always able to reach out to them because they would always be available and they guided me to new and good choices.

They were real solid people. When an associate called me and told me what they had seen, that they'd caught them, Christina and Dwight, I did go into an anger rage. Am I proud of what I did back then? No, I am not. I am now teaching my kids how to solve things differently, but for the most part of the situation, I did end up going to juvenile jail for attempted murder. That's what they gave me, along with two other charges when you deface somebody. She had to get plastic surgery for the cuts that I put on her face, so I went to juvenile for six months. It was supposed to have been juvenile life plus a couple of years after I turned twenty-one, but my boyfriend's mother Ms. Linda came to my defense. I really appreciated her then and now for standing up for me, seeing better in me and not judging me. She saw the situation that I came from. She saw the situation that I was around.

My boyfriend had explained a lot that he even witnessed at the house to his mother and that made her fight hard for me. She and Mr. Kurt, her husband, who was a sergeant while she was an RN. They went to court and got me released under some stipulations. I had to stay out of trouble for five years. I also had to complete therapy programs, see a psychiatrist, get on medication, and take anger management classes. When I was released, it was right before I entered Job Corps. That's when I went to the group home and the state took guardianship.

I had to give you guys the story on how I almost threw my life away at the age of fourteen. I am so thankful that I was allowed a second chance. My mom (Ms. Linda), that's what I call her, believed in me. She saw something in me that other people could not see. She knew that I had come from a bad situation starting young and she pleaded with the judges to give me the opportunity to show them that I could be a better person and I could function in society. I didn't want her vouch for me to be in vain. I didn't want her to put her name on the line and prove the system right that they should've just kept me locked up. So, I got my education and started trying to take the right turns for the better. I worked hard to stay out of trouble and to do what's right.

That's where this story ends up turning back to Job Corps with my friends that were into knowledge, power and 5% studies. They read up on positivity and enlightenment, and I needed that in my life during those moments because I was on a path of destruction and anger. Before getting with my friends, I didn't want anybody talking to me or bothering me. I was like a ticking time bomb, so being around them helped to balance me out and make me focus and think better about the choices I was making during those times. I was able to go to Job Corps with only one incident in hand. I stayed focused, thanks to the teachings and to my friends Amina, Tyrique, Gizelle, and Jamal. I didn't get physical, but words were exchanged in that incident. However, Job Corps pushed it to the side because they saw the effort I had given during my stay. They saw my grades were honors and how I had passed my driving test. I had passed my GED within only one time of taking it. I also was passing in business technology classes, so they decided to keep me in because I had only one incident the whole time.

Wherever Amina and Tyrique went, I went. They knew I didn't have family around like that, so on the holidays they would invite me to go with them for Christmas, Spring Break, Thanksgiving, and any other special vacations. It would be alternate friends, but I loved the fact that they did not want me to be alone for holidays. I really must give it to them for sticking by me and making me feel a part of a family. #US. You all shine bright.

So, my friends in Job Corps all came from different areas, but we all were the same in some ways. Looking for a better way. Trying to progress and start life as an adolescent, preparing for adulthood and trying to find the right path. We hung out a lot. We shared the same ideas as far as our future and our goals, and we knew we wanted to do better in life and have a better life.

Some people would opt into Job Corps to take up a trade. I wanted to study business to go into business for myself. That was my dream at that moment. I did get my business certification from Job Corps, along with my GED and my driver's license. This was all at seventeen. I felt proud of myself because I did accomplish something and I wasn't sitting around wasting my life and getting into trouble. I was very grateful and happy for that. I had made a change. I did something positive and productive for the first time. I'm reaching for the stars.

I also used to struggle with depression because of the abuse that I went through throughout the years of my young life. I had a miscarriage and I didn't realize it was a miscarriage until afterwards. I had just turned thirteen. I went out with this guy that was older than me named Jason or "JJ." I was doing a lot of rebelling and leaving the house to escape the mistreatment and hanging in areas not appropriate for a child my age. Jason was not much older than me and he was always around the area I lived in. We started hanging out when I would skip school. The school I was attending was on the southside and I just didn't have ambition anymore after living with my Aunt Wendy, so I started getting involved in activities again.

Living with the reality of not having a father or a mother to turn to, I just wanted to escape pain whenever I could. My self-esteem issues were sky high being thirteen trying to find my identity. Being called ugly among other hurtful things had me searching for validation and love in places that were tricky and deceitful. I searched even harder for that void to be filled when we moved to Richmond. Having "JJ" pay attention to me and he was older, was like some sort of prize to me, I thought at the time. That's when I didn't know I was pregnant and I went to visit my aunt Veronica for a week in May of '93. My aunt Wendy had taken us to Hampton Roads. We'd normally go over to stay a couple of days. We were upstairs listening to the radio, taking turns singing songs, me, my cousins, and my sisters, and I had to use the bathroom. My stomach was hurting, and I thought it was my menstrual, but when I sat on the toilet, I had pressure so hard, worse than what it normally was. I already had a bad menstruation flow that came on in a way that cramped unbearably. Sometimes it would paralyze me to where I couldn't move, but this was different this time.

I felt something push down hard on the bottom of my stomach. I clenched my legs tightly as I held the screams in from the intense sharp pains shooting up my sides. I was holding onto the sides of the toilet like I was bracing for impact. "I'm in trouble," I thought. Crying, scared, heart pounding outside my body. That's the way I felt. Frozen.

Then something slid from me. I heard a splash. Scared to look, I yelled for Queenie. She came to the door running, almost tripping over her shoelaces. I let Queenie in and told her how much pain I was in and that something was in the toilet. We are both scared, she younger than I, so she goes to get my cousin "Tootsie." When Tootsie comes in to help me because she is older and calmer and more collected, I lean forward so she could see, and I heard both Queenie and Tootsie gasp and run for the door. I cried out "Please, don't leave. I'm in trouble." That's when I heard the toilet flush. I can't remember who flushed it. I was in a daze from shock by then. I squeezed my legs as tight as I could and held my stomach crying in agony. I sat on the toilet for what seemed like a lifetime. I was afraid to get up. I thought something else was going to come out after the first two splashes I heard earlier. I finally got up the courage to get off the toilet. Tootsie had given me sanitary napkins to put in my underwear as we got ready for bed.

We spent the night not saying a word about what happened in the bathroom. We just listened to music while lying there looking out the windows and trying to go to sleep. I was afraid to use the bathroom the rest of the night, fearing it would happen again. We never told anybody, so I never got any medical attention for that miscarriage. We always kept that secret. I honestly think that was the start of me having the issues that I started having in my cervix. My problems with cervical cancer will come later than sooner, but I'll tell you more about my experiences with that in the second book, Black Flower.

I just used to think about the things that I went through and wonder why me? Why at such a young age did I have to experience these situations? The Most High will never give you more than you can bare, I have learned along the way. I used to vent to my friends about it, trying to get some light on why I was treated a certain way, or why was it done to me, but I never could process a logical answer. I've always wondered why I felt like a black sheep. I never felt like I actually belonged and that came from the mistreatment and the isolation that my aunt Wendy had put me through mostly. With the constant rule standing, nobody could interact with me or talk to me, or they were going to be in trouble. I really want to touch bases on things like this because those things have a great effect on you even when you're in adulthood. Mentally, you still think about things that have happened to you and you try to make sure it doesn't happen to your kids. I struggle with that a lot, trying to prevent any of the things that happened to me from happening to my children. I want life to be the best experience it can be for them. Everyone goes through trials and tribulations, however, if I can pass along any knowledge to help my children not choose the wrong decision, I am willing to do so with all efforts.

Let's take a moment to reflect on the moment my journey took me on a path to joining the military at age eighteen after I left Job Corps. Dwight was facing another charge in court, so he was going to be going away for a couple of months. That's when we discussed me joining the military. He wanted to keep me occupied while he was gone, so I wouldn't fall back into getting in trouble and not preparing for my future. I was going to need a place to live and work, and transportation to get around, so I agreed to go ahead and go into the Army while Dwight served his time and we stay encouraging one another to keep strong as time went by. Dwight was going away for some time. I didn't want to go to the military, but I knew it would help me not be on the streets getting into criminal activities. It would beat struggling and trying to survive with nothing. So, I pushed forward and went to MEPS in Richmond. I did all the testing and completed screening. They told me when I was supposed to leave, which was January of that following year, and I believe that was 1999. I started getting restless and nervous about leaving, thinking about what it meant to serve in the military, the importance of signing the papers to enlist in Boot Camp and showing up to Boot Camp on the date assigned. I kept sitting back reading over my papers and what I acknowledged and what I had sworn to and I started second-guessing and thinking like, I can't do this.

I was nervous about the fact that I already had a problem with authority growing up, acting out and being a rebel. I just was thinking about how they were going to be yelling at me, calling me names, and getting in my face spitting with each word they shouted out in commands. No, I didn't think I could condition myself to become like a piece of property to the country, not being able to leave when I wanted but only doing what is "ordered". I knew I could condition myself because I was already a ward of the state having already experienced all of it except the war section. I just didn't want to submit myself to more anguish when I was broken trying to glue the pieces back together. I didn't want to be in the system anymore, so I went back up to the Military Pass station and let them know that I didn't want to join. The opportunity to opt out of enlisting was available as long as it was before you entered into Boot Camp (that is arriving on the date set to enlist and getting on that training bus). They did take my military card and cut it up, of course, but I did not go to the military after all. UP FOR THE LONG ROAD.

Chapter 9: Training Ground

Dwight and I had an efficiency type room in a hotel that we were staying at until we got our own place. He would hustle and always provided by any means, while I was working in the hotels on the oceanfront as a housekeeper. That's something I had been doing off and on throughout the last year. He would be out doing whatever he needed to do to make sure that he could provide for us and keep a roof over our heads. And then one night, late night, his cousins called and wanted to come down and visit from New York. I told him I didn't think it was a good idea. I had a bad feeling and I didn't think they needed to come down at the moment. I already knew how they ran and what they were into, so I just didn't think he needed to take that chance because he was already trying to get through another court charge. He had convinced me it was OK; they were just going to come for a couple of days. The visit was going to be short, they were just stopping through on their way down South. That was the plan. I mean, what could happen in seventy-two hours? Choices. We all have choices.

So, they ended up coming down the next day. The first day was fine. Nothing happened except for them going out all across Hampton Roads, four people to five people in each car (normally two vehicles), visiting other relatives. Then, they came back and I fixed food for everybody. The second day was the worst day of my life because my life really changed after that. It was like I had been given a whole new life, starting back at the bottom. Dwight and his two cousins got dressed about twelve or one o'clock that day. The sun was shining bright and the weather was feeling good; seventy-seven degrees. I think that's normally when he used to get up because he would be out almost most of the night trying to get the money to make sure that we were taken care of. So, they rolled up some smoke and drank a few Heinekens before heading out for the day. He gave me a hug and said he would see me later. We were going to go looking for more apartments the next day. I went on about my day like I normally do, getting myself together for work and making meals to put up in the fridge just in case he came back early. When I got off work, I realized that I hadn't talk to him since my lunch break. He would always call and make sure I made it home from work.

So, I tried to call, but I couldn't get an answer; It was just ringing. Then finally, one of his friends called me and said that he was in jail; he and his two cousins. My stomach twisted in knots, aching. It was like a sledgehammer had impacted with my torso with great force. My body was numb but shaking. I was trying to figure out what was going on. My mind was foggy. Why is he in jail? Why did they get locked up? I couldn't understand. He wouldn't jeopardize everything knowing we were moving at the end of the month and having other court cases. I know he wouldn't, I thought with fury and frustration. I just couldn't make sense of it. I found out why he was being charged because I ended up having to be subpoenaed as a witness since we lived together and I had been with him for five years, off and on. They said they felt I knew something because I was very close to him, so they would have to put me on the stand and question me. I knew nothing. Dwight never let me get involved in anything he was doing in the streets. He wanted me to stay positive and he encouraged knowledge and success. They tried to insinuate things were planned and intentional, but they weren't. Dwight wasn't violent. He wasn't that type of person, but when you hang around the wrong people at the wrong times, you end up getting into things you can't get out of.

Dwight and his cousins were on trial for robbery and assault of military personnel, in which Dwight knew the person. They were acquaintances, but the person that was assaulted didn't know his two cousins at all. His two cousins had decided that they wanted to rob the man, not telling Dwight their plans, he ended up driving them over there because he normally goes over to see him and give him things, so he didn't think anything like that was going to happen. In the spur of the moment, they stabbed Dwight's acquaintance and made him go to the ATM to withdraw money, which that was no success, and that's how they ended up getting caught because he collapsed in the store. Dwight was the driver of the car, so he ended up going to jail, but the military personnel actually testified on his behalf, stating the kind of person he was and that he knew he had nothing to do with the assault and attempted robbery and it wasn't intentional on Dwight's end. The judge said that the acquaintance's testimony on my boyfriend's behalf would be taken into consideration, however my boyfriend didn't want to testify against his cousins, so they charged him as an accomplice to the fact of the crimes. He was facing anywhere from six to ten years or six to fifteen.

At this time, I am eighteen, about to be nineteen, staying in this efficiency room. Dwight was gone now. He'd been sent away for six years and I'm trying to figure out what am I going to do now because he was the main line for me. I relied on him. He was my backbone at that time. I didn't have strength like I have these days. I was still vulnerable, trying to figure things out, learning as I go, stumbling and falling and trying to understand what I needed to do in the world. So, I'm crying, eyes burning and puffy. I had been crying all day. Thinking hard. Trying to make a plan appear. I'm in this room, check out is at the end of the week. I'm trying to figure out how I'm going to get that much money because I didn't make that type of money at the hotels working as a housekeeper to provide for that. Dwight was the one providing for the most part. I would pay the small things like the phone bill, toiletries, my hair extensions and sometimes food. The rent, clothing, transportation, and most of the food came from him. I had three days left before another payment was due for the efficiency room when I ran into a woman named "Queen." I was sitting on the sidewalk having me a drink, even though I knew I wasn't supposed to drink under the age of twenty-one.

Queen started talking to me and asking me what was wrong, and I confided in her my situation. That's when we linked and she said, "I can show you how to make some money, so you don't have to worry." At this moment, I'm like, yeah okay, let me see. I'm open to anything because in a minute, I'm going to be out on the street. I don't have anywhere to go and I can't turn to anybody at this time. I'm going to make it on my own, I vowed. So, I went ahead and saw what she had to offer.

First thing Queen did was give me little lessons on how to be a hostess and dance in a seductive way, giving the dreamy eyes and capturing people's stare when performing. I started learning how to walk in stiletto heels and how to dress up in a very intriguing way to get people to notice me. Once Queen gave me the ABCs of that, I pretty much took off on my own. There was a hotel that used to be out in Virginia that everybody knew was a spot for escorting and other services, parties, and dances, so I started going there and partaking in getting women to do dance shows for men. I became a Madam. I was a Madam at the age of nineteen. When Queen showed me the ropes, I really, really took hold of it. That's when I ran into Shug. He was a pimp also at the hotel working with his girls, and he liked the way I operated, so he decided he wanted to be in partnership with me, which really didn't become a partnership. He was in fact trying to own me at first and have me working for him. Me being naïve and young, I said yes to the business deal. He was older than me, and Queen had vouched for him, so I trusted that business would be business.

I was in charge of the women in the beginning. I would teach them how to dance, how to wear their hair and how to put themselves together in an intriguing but sophisticated manner. I would teach them how to hold an interesting conversation and how to be of good companionship when we would come into contact with dates at gatherings. Shug also had me going out canvassing on the strips at the beach and clubs for new "talent," and also pushing out our flyers for different parties. I did it for a few weeks and then I noticed he was starting to get verbally abusive to not just me, but all of us, being moody, cursing us out and telling us we can't go out without his permission and that we need to be checking in with him at certain times. He even started monitoring our phones. He had two bodyguards (Zeus and Big Ron) that started staying by the doors or chaperoned us wherever he sent us. I said to myself, "I have to figure a way out of this. I have to think of a plan." I was ready to fight for myself, protect myself and fight for my freedom from any anything and anyone. I had suffered so much from all the abuse in my life. I had already gone through drastic times from the age of eight. So, after listening to him be verbally abusive with threats of what he was going to do, even though he never got physically abusive with us but it was a lot of verbal, a light beamed in my head, bright as the sun on a July beach day. I had to hurry. Do it tonight. I wasn't going to get a second chance. That's the fear I had keeping me strapped down. The way Shug would wave those guns at us and have Zeus and Big Ron standing behind us, it literally did scare everyone, and no one would move or stay out late or not contact Shug when told because we didn't know whether Shug was bluffing or not. He hadn't hurt us physically, but we knew of what he could to others.

Later that night, I was talking to the women in the house as we were preparing dinner together. We would make each other's favorite meal, taking turns each day of the week. I told them, "I'm not going to submit myself to more abuse again after everything I've endured over time." I asked them to meet in the downstairs room where our radio and entertainment center was. Playing music as we so often did while painting our toes and grooming ourselves, I said, "I'm leaving tonight. I don't know who wants to come with me, but I'm not going to stay another night in here. We are bringing in the cash, doing all the work and get abused at the same time. I think not." I turned the radio up just a notch more with Foxy Brown playing and said, "So, if you want to come with me, pack your things. We leave in an hour." Shug was in the bed sleep with the flu. He had told Zeus and Big Ron they didn't have to stay that day because we weren't leaving the house because he was sick. As we were packing, I wanted to assure them it wasn't going to be the same coming along with me. I said, "I will still show you the ropes and keep shelter and food for everyone. I'm not going to stress the issue as far as you better check in with me and you can't go anywhere or talk to anyone as Shug did. I want to keep us happy so we can stack up the dough and get where we need to be. No drama. All respect and trust." I was making all the major moves as far as connecting with the right source to have us live comfortable enough to pay for shelter, food, and toiletries, and to have money to play in the field with. We were going to be working like a solid team. I let the girls know that when they came with me, all they had to give was something for our phone bills, fragrance and makeup collections and contributions toward getting items to liven up our place. Whatever else they made, they kept. A certain percentage was also given to me for finding the people and organizing a party and travel expenses. Out of the fifteen girls he had, I think it was nine of them that went with me.

All nine of them decided to pack that night. Shug was going north somewhere anyway later that night for a money pickup and we were supposed to stay at home. So, when he left, I waited, I'll say about thirty to forty-five minutes after he pulled off before we made our exit. We grabbed our belongings and caught a cab over to another hotel facility in the next city. I checked us in, and we stayed there for a couple of weeks. During that couple weeks timeframe, Shug was searching around the cities. He was upset and looking for us because I had taken most of the girls with me. He was looking around for us in all the local areas we normally frequented. When he finally found us, it had been months and we weren't going back. I was doing well with the girls. We were "independent" now, I would say. I let Shug know that we were doing our own thing now. We didn't work for nobody and we were surviving just fine with our arrangement. The girls and I wanted to be in control of our paths. That's when the tension and animosity came between me and Shug because I took his women with me and started my own thing and he didn't appreciate that. A short time after the run-in with Shug at the club, he tried to sabotage me in a way that was very dangerous to all of us.

I knew some people in New York, both family and friends, that were in business in every borough, but he knew the connections for these dance clubs that we would take the girls to. So, even though I knew Shug had bad blood for me because I had taken in most of the girls, I still took his advice on meeting up with another person for business. All the girls and I went up to New York to link with Shug's connect (Rob B) at his club. After meeting with Rob B, touring the clubs and seeing the places we would be renting while in the city, I thought it would be a good idea to take them up that way to make more money.

We came back to Virginia the next day to pack and arrange for our stay in New York for the rest of the winter. All of us chasing the same goal. Stack the money, get a place, and start a legitimate job. We all were trying to settle down somewhere and leave the dangerous streets. Later that night, the girls and I set off for New York on the bus. When we arrived, Rob B picked us up from the downtown Manhattan Port Authority. We went over to a house he had in Brooklyn and there he gave me the rundown of where we were going to go later. Rob B told me what club we were going to and asked what girls I wanted to perform for the first night. I showed him which two were going to be performing the first night and everybody else was going to get to know the area and get settled in with their charm. All of a sudden, the girls and I get to the club so I can introduce them and things get a little shaky and fishy. I got a bad feeling. I was sensing something. My stomach went into knots. Rob B and his driver locked the doors to the truck. His driver smirked and said, "Got the child lock on the doors. You can't get out." Then, Rob B started speaking with a strong, conquering tone saying, "I own you now. You work for me and you're not going back to Virginia."

"I'm a Madame. You can't own me and you can't take these girls. They are with me," I said in a surprised but stern voice. I asked, "So, we not going by the code, huh?" (Rob B clicked the safety off the gun). "Ok, ok. I see how this is." I told my girls to get out of the car and go to the club as we'd planned. I assured them it was going to be alright, but I knew this was the beginning of us having to put our survival skills to use.

Rob B had his nephew take me back to his house because I was supposed to be waiting for the first two girls to finish their performance at the club. While I am sitting in Rob B's nephew's living room, I started zoning out the conversation he was having with his girlfriend.

They were watching the game on tv and drinking Grey Goose, talking about what was going to be happening the next day. I sat there for the rest of the night thinking about how I needed to get out of the house. No phone call from Rob B and I couldn't get in touch with the girls because his nephew had taken my phone. Then, the sun rose and I hear a phone ring in the back bedroom. His nephew is talking so low, I couldn't hear the conversation. I sit up as the door opens to the bedroom. His nephew hands over the phone. Rob B is talking in a pleasant, but sarcastic voice now. He's still telling me on the phone how I wasn't getting any of the women back because I worked for him now. All of my things, like my jewels and my important papers I had in my luggage, was at his other house. My GED, my birth certificate, all of that; I had all my belongings in one bag.

That's just how I lived during those moments. I didn't have a lot, so I asked Rob B could I get my things back. I was like, "You really think that I'm going to work for you? I've always been a little stubborn and hardheaded and played around with fire more than I care to share." Rob B, now yelling on the phone, began saying, "No, you're not getting anything back. I'm gonna send somebody to come get you in a minute." He was telling me what I was going to be doing now that I worked for him.

After I got off the phone with him, I'm sitting there like," I have to think quick. They are coming." I'm looking out the window at an escape. They are not going to let me leave and I am not going to be nobody's walker. So I'm contemplating in my head, I have an ex-boyfriend who stays in Queens. I still know his number because we're still cool. We never had any issues with each other as far as a bad separation. He got locked up and I had to move out of state. After that, we lost touch. I called him and I said, "Listen, I'm here with my girls because I was under the impression that I could bring them up here to try to make some money at these clubs. But now, this pimp is trying to turn me into one of his girls, and you know that ain't happening." He said, "What are you going to do?" I told him I was going to ask for something to eat. I knew there was no food there because his nephew's girlfriend was saying they needed more food in the house. I went to the bedroom door and knocked. She came to the door with some clothes in her hand. I took the clothing, a black jean skirt with a see-through shirt and bathing suit. I said thank you, then asked for something to eat. She said there was a bodega on the corner I could get a hoagie from and that I could change in the bathroom, so I go in there and I slip it into my outfit. It was cold, but I had to make a run for it. I could think about warmth later. At least the weather was in the 70s, the newscaster said earlier on the TV. I had on heels, no sneakers, I did not even have my ID because all of that was left in my suitcase at his house. I grabbed the wad of money that was on the dresser and acted like I didn't know how to get to the bodega. The nephew's girlfriend gave me another twenty-dollar bill and put in an order to bring back.

So, after telling them I didn't know where it was, they showed me because I wasn't for sure if I would be able to get back, but I knew exactly where it was. My mom that raised me, Ms. Linda, was from Brooklyn. She and Grandma Naomi used to be out in those areas where we actually were, but I wasn't gonna tell them that. They told me how to get to the corner store and they let me out the back door so no one would see me leave the house. I walked calmly down that sidewalk with my heels getting stuck in the cracked cement. As soon as I hit the corner, I sprinted. I ran so fast in those heels. I ran like a dog was biting on the back of my heels and I didn't look back not one time. I finally reached a payphone, they had quarter payphones back then, and I called my friend and told him I was down the street from the wholesale store near the train. I said, "I'm about to go in here and get me a fake ID made." At those times, you could go to a store and get a fake ID made in those bodega spots. So, I got an ID made and then I caught the train to downtown Manhattan and got a room in a nice hotel. Instead of going to the low- priced motels, I went to an upscale room over in the secured areas with security. I picked a random, high-class hotel that they wouldn't think I would be at. My friend met me up there and he was like, "You know what, you'll have to lay low for a minute because you know they going to be at the Port Authority trains, airplanes and buses." Rob B was sending his people for me. I contacted my people back home, a couple of my acquaintances I ran in the streets with and let them know that he had taken the girls and was trying to take me over, but I wasn't having it. One of my peoples from back in VA asked where the girls were, and I was like, "Back at his house, I believe. I hadn't seen them since we first arrived and split up." The other two went to the club to perform. I'm sure he took them back to the house, so basically, he did get the girls from me because I couldn't get them back. I was up there by myself now. Me and my friend were figuring out how to get me back to Virginia. I waited about a week and then I got on the bus with the ID I had made at the store. Rob B was still looking for me when I got home. Word had traveled back to VA. Rob B and his boys started calling my peoples and asking them if they had seen me. They must have gotten the information for my people from a source that knew them also. My acquaintances were telling them they hadn't seen me because they thought I was still in New York, but the whole time I'm looking out my friend's window right at them. They were posted up in the parking lot, two cars deep at a hotel across the street. I could see three people to a car. They left after being in VA for almost a week with no info on where I was. Another bullet dodged.

I ended up going down toward Virginia Beach and spending some time with my little cousins that I was close to. I liked to have them with me when I was around long enough to do things with them. This particular warm and bright day, I decided to take them with me for the day. I was going to the studio this day because I liked to write poetry and lyrics. Music is and was therapeutic to me and writing rhymes and lyrics was exciting. Pouring out thoughts and turning them into art was priceless for me back then. Something positive, I would say. Music brings everyone together. I liked to rhyme, and I liked to do a lot of writing. Writing out my feelings and thoughts was something I'd learned in the programs I was in after I was released from juvenile jail. I learned how to express myself by writing freely, cautiously, and with words. So, I was in the studio with the people that I knew produced beats and put together CDs. We were working on a mixer of beats.

We all were affiliated in the same profession, having girls escort services or dance performances for gentlemen, we were in the same business of entertaining. They were some of the top dogs in North Carolina that came down once in a while to make music and conduct other business along the way. As we were getting in the groove in the studio putting some lines down, one of my good friends was recording when we heard someone at the door.

The person had on black leather clothing, black gloves, black boots and was tall and dark. I immediately already knew who he was. It was Zeus, one of the bodyguards working for Shug. He said to the person that owned the studio, "I need to talk to her for a minute." The owner of the studio had known Shug from New York years back before he moved to Virginia. The owner told Shug we was up at the studio dropping lines down and Shug went back and told Rob B where I was because he knew that word in the streets was they were looking for me. When Zeus came in, he had something behind his back. I remember my good friend from North Carolina said, "What's going on? Hold up, stop, we ain't gonna do none of this. This is a female. You know down south is very hospitable." He just couldn't understand what Zeus was trying to do to a young lady. That's when I pulled "North Carolina" in the office and told him everything that happened in New York. And when "North Carolina" heard that, he told him straight up, "You violating. You know it's rules to this." He had his bodyguards come from the back and stand at the doorway. "North Carolina" said in a stern, agitated voice, "We're not gonna do nothing like this. You guys know the rules to this game, and you know you cannot turn a Madame into a walker. She paid her dues, and already has her credibility and you know you're crossing the line." He then shouted in rage, "On top of it, you took all her belongings that belong to her that none of ya paid for. So, she did what she had to do as far as getting herself back home and providing for herself because Rob B took all of her stuff." "North Carolina" then reached for his luggage in the chair behind him.

He asked how much was it that I had taken. I told him the price, roughly four grand and he went in his luggage and got out large bills. He told Zeus, "Look, give this to your people. I don't wanna hear anything else about this in the streets because y'all violated the loyalty and the rules. We take not respecting the game to the heart where I'm from." Zeus got on the phone with Shug and it was over. An angel must be shielding me from all harm. He saved my life that day. If it wasn't for him, I would've been gone. Zeus looked at me and said, "You are a brave young woman. You have that fire and respect." After that, he turned around and walked out the door and I never heard or saw anything about them again. Of course, I was very paranoid for months thereafter thinking that eventually they still were going to try to take me out, but it never happened. So, I felt like "North Carolina" was a guardian angel watching over me. I wasn't by myself, my little cousins were present and that would've been tragic for them repeating the cycle of violence, pain, and trauma, as we all know too well. I have so many more experiences from my youth of stumbling, tripping, falling up that valley and trying to reach the mountain top that I would like to discuss. However, that will take ages. The studio incident wisened me up quicker than ever. It shook me deep in the core. I had a brush with death more than once in the last five years of my life. Time for a change. I knew I was destined for something. I had to find out what it was. Everyone has a destiny.

I'll take you back to the day I showed up on my sister Queenie's door after leaving Shymeek in 2002. I was staying with my sister Queenie in her two bedroom apartment with my niece Roselina. I called her Rosie. She was two years old. I had gotten a job at an overnight warehouse with my friend Leena quality checking car parts. She was working the night-shift there and got me the job. One day, Leena was off from the job, and she stopped pass my sister's house before I left for work. She told me she was going on a date over the weekend and wanted to know if I wanted to double date. I had been back in Virginia for two months now and hadn't gone out at all. I stayed focus, working at night, working a second job during the day, part-time, saving up for a place to rent. I didn't want to overstay my welcome, even though my sister didn't hesitate to open her doors to me. She had her family, her husband and daughter to see after and I didn't want to impose on that. She always would come to my aid when we got older.

I was debating on getting back on the dating scene after what I encountered with Shymeek. The thought of how things ended up in the relationship had set a bitter taste for me. Leena eventually talked me into dinner and drinks with her date and his cousin, Nathan. When Nathan was introduced, he called himself "Nate." Nathan was slim, quiet, and laid-back. I wanted something different, slow- paced, no drama. At the time, Nathan was a great start in that direction. We hit it off and began dating. He was staying with his mother, Grace at the time of our introduction. She was sophisticated, stylish, and laid- back like Nathan. Grace would welcome me to events she would have. She cooked amazing food, also. And she knew how to have a great party with laughter, dancing, and peace. After dating Nathan for a few months, we both saved up enough for our own place in Norfolk. It wasn't huge and fancy, but it was a start. It was a nice, one bedroom apartment ten minutes away from the mall and downtown. Nathan worked at an asphalt company while I was still working at the warehouse with Leena. When Nathan and I moved in together, it was like turning a new page. No marks or blemishes. The first month was wonderful. We would get off work, go on dates, double date, and go to family dinners at his mother's house at least once a week. After a while, I began to notice a pattern with Nathan. I didn't really pay attention in the beginning because he had won me over. Charm isn't the word. He brought chivalry back. He began staying out late, even coming home in the mornings. I questioned the reason and his response would be he was playing pool and sometimes he would say he slept at his mother's house. At first, I didn't question it. I trusted him. He had never given a sign to me that I couldn't. The late nights got later, and I was starting to wonder if I was blind-sided by the positive interactions with Nathan and the kind and gentle treatment he was giving me. By then, my younger sister Raven had come to stay with me for a while. My sister Queenie and I had been taking care of her and getting her through school because my mother Deloris still hadn't changed her habits. She mainly stayed with Queenie, but for now she was with me.

After three nights of the same pattern Nathan was projecting on me, coming home drunk, coming home three to four in the morning, and taking late-night private phone calls, I caught him cheating. I woke up as the sun rose over the building to an empty bed. I put my shoes on and went outside to sit at the bottom of the stairs. An hour went by. It was now seven in the morning. Nathan pulls up and walks toward me with a "I-Know-I-Messed-Up" look on his face and says, "I was at my mom's house drinking and playing pool with my cousin and brother. I passed out." I got up and went in the house cursing, crying, and yelling, "I know you wasn't at your mother's house all night." I went in the house and called Mrs. Grace. She was an upfront kind of person. She didn't hold no punches when it came to anything. Mrs. Grace spoke the truth how it was. She told me Nathan had left her house early. She thought he went home. I had my answer. It was nothing to question anymore. It was clear, it was someone else. I got dressed and went to work knowing what I must do. That night while Nathan was asleep, I awoke my sister Raven and told her I was leaving. I told her to go to school in the morning and go to Queenie's house after school. I gave her my house key to get back in (she went to school from my house at that time). She would wait for my sister to pick her up after school and bring her back in the mornings.

She helped me pack my luggage quietly, trying not to make sound. Nathan was still sleep. I told her I was catching a cab to the Greyhound and I would call when I got back up North. It was a hard decision. I had a new life, stress and drama free, no chaos or bad influences around. However, I was being lied to and betrayed again. The trust was broken. By the time Nathan wakes and realizes I have packed my things and gone, I will be miles away, starting over again.

My heart was broken. I cried with deep pain piercing through my soul as I left my sisters again and the person I thought was perfect for me. The image of love and happiness withers away as I try to make sense of it and start my journey in another direction. Another path I must walk to find my purpose.

Afterword

This has been a journey to live through and I appreciate you journeying with me on this read. This is just the beginning as I seek to share but also empower the one that sees no purpose in all that they have gone through and even why. I'm not bitter or judgmental against my story, hence being freely able to share. I want to encourage you that even though you may be in an uphill valley experience, you can find peace. Rest in solace in your mountain experience.

Bless, Tasha M!

www.ingramcontent.com/pod-product-compliance
Lightning Source LLC
Chambersburg PA
CBHW072050160426
43197CB00014B/2708